West Front

House

Senate

# Cornerstones of Freedom

# The Story of
# THE POWERS
# OF CONGRESS

By R. Conrad Stein

Illustrated by Keith Neely

CHILDRENS PRESS ®

CHICAGO

# Newsweek

WATERGATE

Library of Congress Cataloging in Publication Data

Stein, R. Conrad,
   The powers of Congress.

   (Cornerstones of freedom)
   Summary: Discusses the role of Congress in
governmental separation of powers, defines the powers
and rights held by Congress, and examines how the
balance of power between President and Congress has
shifted in the last two centuries.
   1.   United States. Congress—Powers and duties—
Juvenile literature.   [1.   United States. Congress—
Powers and duties.   2.   Separation of powers]
I.   Title.   II   Series.
JK1064.S73   1985        328.73'074        85-10943
ISBN 0-516-04695-0              AACR2

On a sultry afternoon in August, 1974, three grim-faced members of the United States Congress entered President Richard Nixon's office in the White House. They were Senators Hugh Scott and Barry Goldwater and Representative John Rhodes. All three were Republicans, members of the president's own party. The meeting had been called as a result of the American people's outrage over the shocking Watergate scandal. Every day there seemed to be new evidence pointing to the president's apparent involvement in the cover-up of a bungled burglary that took place two years earlier at a Democratic party office in the Watergate Hotel. Now an angry Congress was preparing to remove the president from office through the process called impeachment.

After a few minutes of small talk, Senator Goldwater told Nixon that he lacked the votes in the Senate to avoid impeachment. Senator Scott agreed. Rhodes claimed that members of the House of Representatives also favored impeachment.

"It's grave," said Scott.

"Hopeless," added Goldwater.

Nixon thanked the men for coming and told them he would decide on his next move soon. Two days

later, the president spoke to the nation on television: "Throughout the long and difficult period of Watergate, I have felt it was my duty. . .to complete the term of office to which you elected me. In the past few days, however, it has become evident to me that I no longer have a strong enough political base in Congress. . . ." Later in the speech Nixon announced, "Therefore I shall resign the presidency effective at noon tomorrow."

Although the resignation was expected, the words still stunned the millions of television viewers.

Never before had a president resigned from office. The American president is probably the most powerful man on earth. Yet the Congress, threatening to exercise its own power of impeachment, forced him out of office in disgrace. The Nixon resignation is a historic example of the powers of Congress.

The powers held by the two houses of Congress were first spelled out in the American Constitution. That document was written two centuries ago by the remarkable Constitutional Convention. Some of the most famous of the country's founding fathers attended the convention in Philadelphia. The delegates included George Washington, Benjamin Franklin, James Madison, and Alexander Hamilton.

Establishing a Congress was a major task for the convention. Ideally, a Congress is a lawmaking body composed of individual representatives chosen by voters in their home states.

At the convention, an argument developed over how many representatives each state should have in the new Congress. Large states, led by Virginia, wanted the number of representatives to be based on population alone. States with smaller populations, such as New Jersey, wanted all states to have the same number of representatives. A compromise was struck when the delegates agreed to create a Congress with two bodies—the Senate and the House of Representatives. In the Senate, each state would have two representatives, while in the House, a state would have a number of representatives based on its population.

The delegates also created an office of the president and a court system. The possible rise of a dictator was a lingering fear in their minds. A decade earlier, they had fought a war against the dictatorial king of England. So, as a built-in safeguard against dictatorship, they split the government into three branches: the executive branch (the office of the president), the legislative branch (the Congress), and the judicial branch (the court system headed by the Supreme Court). It was hoped that each branch would serve as a check on the power of the others. Today the system of divided authority is called the separation of powers.

Clearly, the writers of the Constitution intended the lion's share of federal power to go to the Congress. Among the powers given to Congress were the right to tax, the right to spend money, the right to borrow, and the right to declare war. The Constitution also spelled out how a bill becomes a law. Here, too, the convention gave Congress the advantage. After a proposed law is approved by Congress, it is sent to the president for his signature of approval. If the president is displeased with the bill, he may veto it (refuse to approve it). However, the Constitution gives Congress the authority to override a presidential veto. With a two-thirds vote from both the House and the Senate, the bill becomes a law despite the veto.

When the Constitutional Convention finally adjourned, the delegates believed they had created a government with divided authority, but one that would be dominated by Congress. Yet today, it is the president who makes the bold moves, commands the headlines, and generally leads the nation. A famous Constitutional authority, Professor James MacGregor Burns, says: "In its actual exercise of power Congress has lost out to its great rival, the president, who in many respects holds today the commanding place in our national government that the founding fathers intended Congress to have."

How did the president end up with the leadership position the writers of the Constitution hoped to give to the Congress? Largely through a process that lawyers call Constitutional development. In practice, the Constitution was not looked upon as words carved in stone like some ancient religious creed. Instead, the Constitution changed, or developed, as the decades passed. Often the office of the president proved to be better able than Congress to carry out certain duties. Consequently, some power shifted away from Congress to the president.

One of the reasons for the dominance of the executive over the legislative branch was the president's capacity to make swift decisions. Although the president may employ a large staff of advisers, the ultimate decision on a matter is up to him alone. Congress, on the other hand, must hold a vote to provide a resolution to a problem. The vote is usually preceded by time-consuming debates. As a critic once said, "The Congress doesn't run—it waltzes."

Early in the nation's history, the president's office demonstrated its greater efficiency over Congress. According to the Constitution, treaties must be made with the "advice and consent" of the Senate. In 1790, President George Washington went to the Senate hoping to get its opinions on a proposed treaty. Instead of giving Washington the advice he sought, the senators argued among themselves and finally voted to postpone their recommendations. George Washington became furious. According to one senator, "The president of the United States started up in a violent fret [and said], 'This defeats every purpose in my coming here!'" With that, Washington stormed out of the Senate chambers. Since then, no president has asked the Senate for its "advice" before entering a treaty with a foreign power. Thus, the Congress lost an important influence on the direction of the nation's foreign affairs. It can consent (or refuse to do so) only *after* a treaty has been signed.

Certainly the most important single power a government branch can have is the authority to wage war. Here the Constitution gives one direction to the Congress and another to the executive. Article One says, "The Congress shall have power to declare war...." But a clause in Article Two reads, "The President shall be Commander-in-Chief of the Army and Navy...." Today this is interpreted to

mean that the president can order troops, airplanes, and ships to any part of the world to defend the interests of the United States. So, a president can wage war without waiting for Congress to make an actual declaration of war. The bloody conflicts in both Korea and Vietnam were presidential wars. In neither case was the Congress asked to declare war.

The war in Vietnam severely divided the American people. Hoping to prevent future presidential wars, the Congress passed the War Powers Act in 1973. This act negates the president's commander-in-chief clause by asserting an important power of Congress—the power over the purse. The

JOHN C. CALHOUN

HENRY CLAY

JAMES
MADISON

Constitution gives Congress the exclusive right to raise taxes and spend public money. The War Powers Act declares that Congress can refuse to spend money to support any prolonged presidential war. It remains to be seen whether the War Powers Act will prevent another conflict like the one in Vietnam.

Since the American government's beginnings, the powers of Congress have risen and fallen in contrast to the strength of the president. Generally, during peacetime the power of Congress tends to increase while the president's authority diminishes. In wartime the reverse takes place. Also, the twentieth century has seen an era of strong presidents and comparatively weak legislatures.

The nineteenth century was the heyday of powerful Congresses. Early in the 1800s, a group of young frontiersmen headed by Henry Clay and John C. Calhoun began to dominate Congress. Because they favored war with Great Britain, they were called the "War Hawks." At that time, Congress was powerful enough to lead the nation into war. The influence of the War Hawks pushed a cautious President James Madison into acts that mushroomed into the War of 1812.

DANIEL WEBSTER

SAM HOUSTON

In the decades following that war, the issue of slavery and its expansion into new states commanded the country's attention. The halls of Congress rang with fiery debates that sometimes exploded into fistfights. At the time, Congress included such notables as Daniel Webster of Massachusetts and Sam Houston of Texas. In the troubled years leading up to the Civil War, Americans focused their attention on the activities of Congress while the office of the president took a back seat.

16

The domination of Congress over the affairs of the country ended with the first cannonballs fired over Fort Sumter. The Civil War was the most destructive conflict ever fought by Americans. While that bloody war raged, President Abraham Lincoln grabbed powers traditionally held by Congress. At the start of the fighting, he expanded the army without waiting for congressional approval. He spent money never appropriated by Congress. In an effort to suppress southern sympathizers, he suspended civil rights. Congressional leaders simply looked the other way while the president stripped away their time-honored authority.

FORT SUMTER

ABRAHAM LINCOLN

THE RADICAL REPUBLICANS

After the Civil War, Congress reasserted its powers. In fact, Congress exercised its ultimate weapon against the president—the power to impeach.

A group called the Radical Republicans held sway over Congress at war's end. In the Senate, they were led by Charles Sumner of Massachusetts and in the House by a feisty old Pennsylvanian named Thaddeus Stevens. The Radical Republicans wanted to punish the Confederacy by placing large sections of the South under prolonged military rule. Serving in the White House was Andrew Johnson, a

Democrat who had been Lincoln's vice-president. He hoped to carry out Lincoln's policy of restoring the Union "with malice toward none, with charity for all." The stage was set for the most dramatic clash between legislative and executive authority in the nation's history.

Claiming that President Johnson had violated congressional laws, the Radical Republicans moved to impeach him. So confident were the Radicals of their own strength, and of the powers of Congress, that Thaddeus Stevens said, "No government official from the president and the chief justice down, can do any one act which is not prescribed and directed by legislative power."

Following rules laid down in the Constitution, impeachment proceedings began in the House of Representatives. The word *impeach* means to accuse. To remove a president from his office, the House must first impeach (accuse) him of committing a crime. Then the Senate must hold a trial to determine whether or not the president is guilty of that crime. In February, 1868, the House of Representatives elected to impeach Andrew Johnson by a vote of 126 to 47. The proceedings then moved to the Senate, where conviction required a two-thirds vote.

The Senate galleries buzzed with spectators as the clash between the president and the Congress continued. Emotions boiled and tempers flared. A senator from Maine received a letter saying, "Any Republican senator who is against impeachment need never expect to get home alive." But soon it became clear that the Radical Republicans had a weak case against the president. At the end of the trial, Johnson was acquitted by one vote. Many experts on the Constitution believe the acquittal saved the presidency from becoming a weak office that would forever be subordinate to Congress.

The second half of the 1800s continued to see strong Congresses. But there were no more history-making conflicts with the executive branch. Instead, the country's amazing economic growth commanded the attention of the people. Then came the twentieth century and the advent of total war.

During wars of great commitment, such as World War I and World War II, the country rallied behind its presidents. A collective body such as Congress simply could not provide the personal leadership the people sought in those times of crisis. Professor James MacGregor Burns claims that during the two wars the president became "a sort of Constitutional dictator." In World War I, Congress gave President Wilson the authority to take over mines and factories. In World War II, Congress was equally

WOODROW WILSON

generous to President Franklin D. Roosevelt. His office was allowed to control prices and set factory quotas.

In the modern era, the experience of total war has done much to strengthen the executive at the cost of legislative authority. However, Congress still

FRANKLIN DELANO ROOSEVELT

RONALD REAGAN

zealously guards some of its powers. A well-pub-
licized example of the legislative branch asserting
its authority over the executive is the annual contest
that newspapers like to call the "battle of the
budget."

The authority to spend public money is one of the
basic powers granted to the Congress by the Constitution. Therefore, once a year, the president must
*ask* Congress for a budget to run the huge executive
department. This includes billions of dollars needed
to fund the military. The president's budget request
is often at odds with the wishes of Congress. The
budget battles waged during the mid-1980s serve as
an example. President Ronald Reagan claimed it
was necessary to spend money on ships, missiles, and
tanks. Many of his opponents in Congress main-

tained that the public money would be better spent on education or social programs.

Compromises in the budget are usually worked out between the president and the Congress before the budget bill is sent to the White House. Once the president receives a proposed budget, he has only two choices—he can accept all of it or reject all of it. By law he cannot approve one part of a bill and veto another part. Sometimes, when the president and the Congress cannot agree on a bill, the country is forced to manage without a budget.

The president is Congress's major Constitutional rival, but not its only one. The separation of powers system also includes the judicial department, which is headed by the Supreme Court.

A professor in Great Britain once told his class that in the United States the Supreme Court has the right to strike down an act of Congress if the Court believes the act violates the Constitution. The class spent the entire night studying the American Constitution. Finally, they concluded that their professor was mistaken. The British students could find nothing in the U.S. Constitution that gave the Supreme Court the authority to overrule an act of Congress.

The British students were both right and wrong. It is true that no words in the Constitution give the Supreme Court authority over acts of Congress. Yet the Supreme Court has held that power since 1803. How the judicial branch acquired its leverage over Congress is another example of Constitutional development.

JOHN MARSHALL

A landmark Supreme Court case called *Marbury* v. *Madison* was settled in 1803. In that case, a brilliant chief justice named John Marshall declared, "A legislative act contrary to the Constitution is not a law." He added, "It is emphatically the province and duty of the judicial department to say what the law is." Simply stated, Justice Marshall argued that someone must determine precisely what the Constitution means, and it is usually judges—not congressmen or presidents—who interpret laws.

The case of *Marbury* v. *Madison* established a practice called judicial review. That means that anyone who feels that an act of Congress violates the Constitution can take a case before the Supreme Court. If the Court agrees, the act becomes void even though it was passed by the Congress and signed by the president.

Judicial review has led to dozens of clashes between Congress and the Supreme Court. During the industrial age of the late 1800s and early 1900s, many congressional acts designed to regulate big business were struck down by a conservative Supreme Court. The Court voided even those laws that forbade child labor.

A historic clash between Congress, the president, and the Supreme Court happened during the Great Depression of the 1930s when the Court overturned acts of Congress meant to ease the sufferings of poor people. These acts were supported by President Franklin D. Roosevelt. A frustrated Roosevelt sponsored a bill that would increase the number of Supreme Court justices from nine to at least fifteen. Since the president appoints all Supreme Court justices, Roosevelt reasoned that he could pack the Court with members who would be sympathetic to his legislation. Moreover, the bill would violate no law since the Constitution does not state how many

THE UNITED STATES SENATE

justices should sit on the Court. But a strange phenomenon occurred when Congress considered Roosevelt's "court-packing" bill. The members of Congress refused to support the bill because they believed that the Supreme Court *should* limit legislative power. Judicial review, in the opinion of most congressmen, was too important for the system of separation of powers to be lost in political squabbles.

The examination of the powers of Congress is a complicated but fascinating study. For two hundred years, lawyers, judges, and scholars have debated the rights and restrictions of congressional authority. Enough books on the matter have been written to fill a library.

Despite the enormously complex issues surrounding its authority, the Congress will always be the voice of the American people. The Capitol Building, with its majestic dome that towers over Washington, is the nation's meeting hall. For more than a century and a half, the stately building has been the site of congressional debates that made history. It is no wonder that Thomas Jefferson once called Congress "the great commanding theater of this nation."

THE UNITED STATES CAPITOL

About the Author

R. Conrad Stein was born and grew up in Chicago. He enlisted in the Marine Corps at the age of eighteen and served for three years. He then attended the University of Illinois where he received a bachelor's degree in history. He later studied in Mexico, earning an advanced degree from the University of Guanajuato. Mr. Stein is the author of many other books, articles, and short stories written for young people.

Mr. Stein now lives in Chicago with his wife, Deborah Kent, who is also a writer of books for young readers, and their daughter Janna.

About the Artist

Keith Neely attended the School of the Art Institute of Chicago and received a Bachelor of Fine Arts degree with honors from the Art Center College of Design where he majored in illustration. He has worked as an art director, designer, and illustrator and has taught advertising illustration and advertising design at Biola College in La Mirada, California. Mr. Neely is currently a freelance illustrator whose work has appeared in numerous magazines, books, and advertisements. He lives with his wife and five children in Florida.